You color to relax - forget your stress - revive your spirit. When you feel tension - color. Just like taking deep breaths and meditation, coloring releases the tensions that form in our bodies. Color just to color! Once you start, you may find a new found "love"! Any patterns bring you peace and joy? Frame It!

Let Go and Relax
Be More Productive in Everything You Do
Make Life Richer through Relaxation Coloring!

I0468902

Animals Coloring Book
DESIGNS

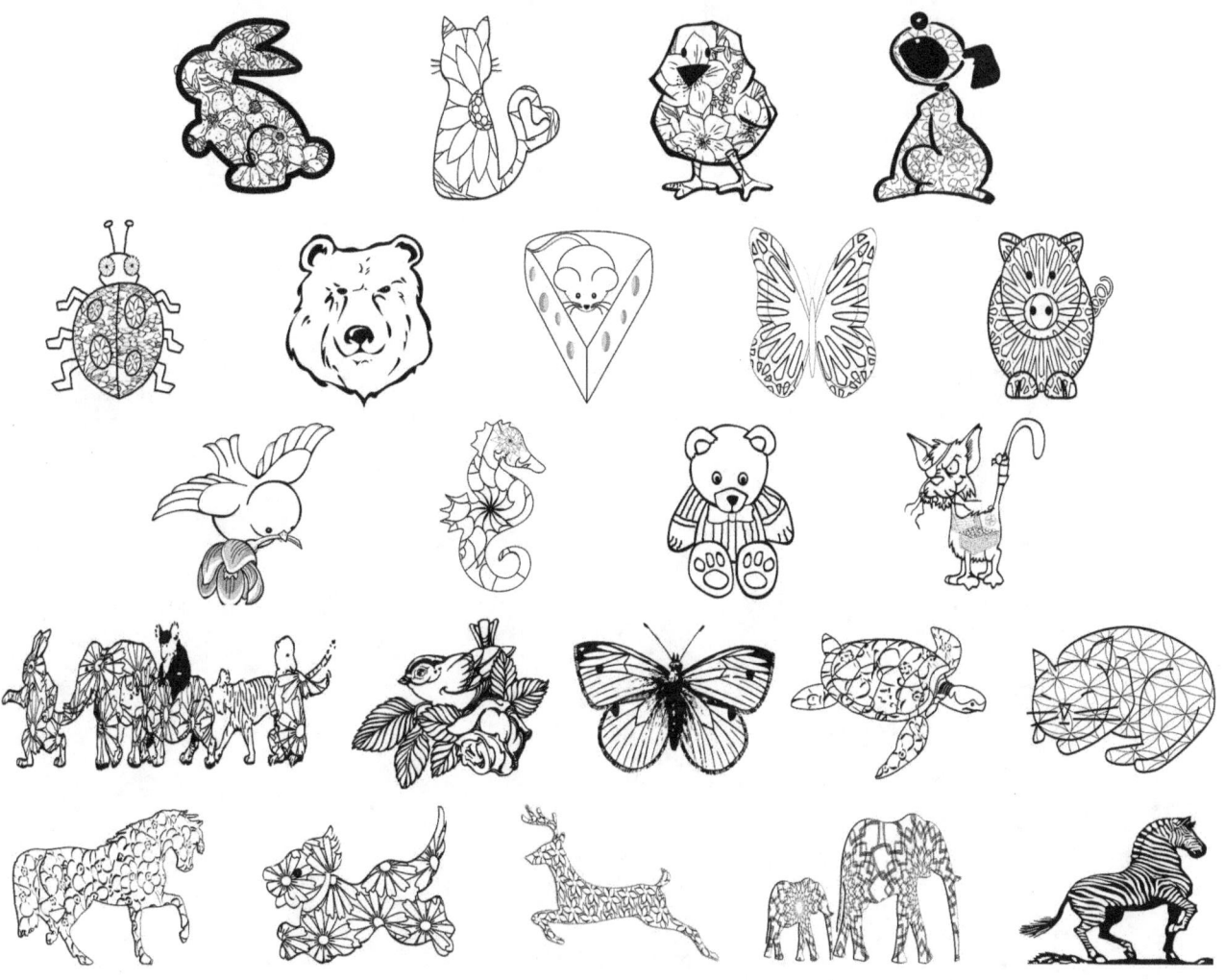

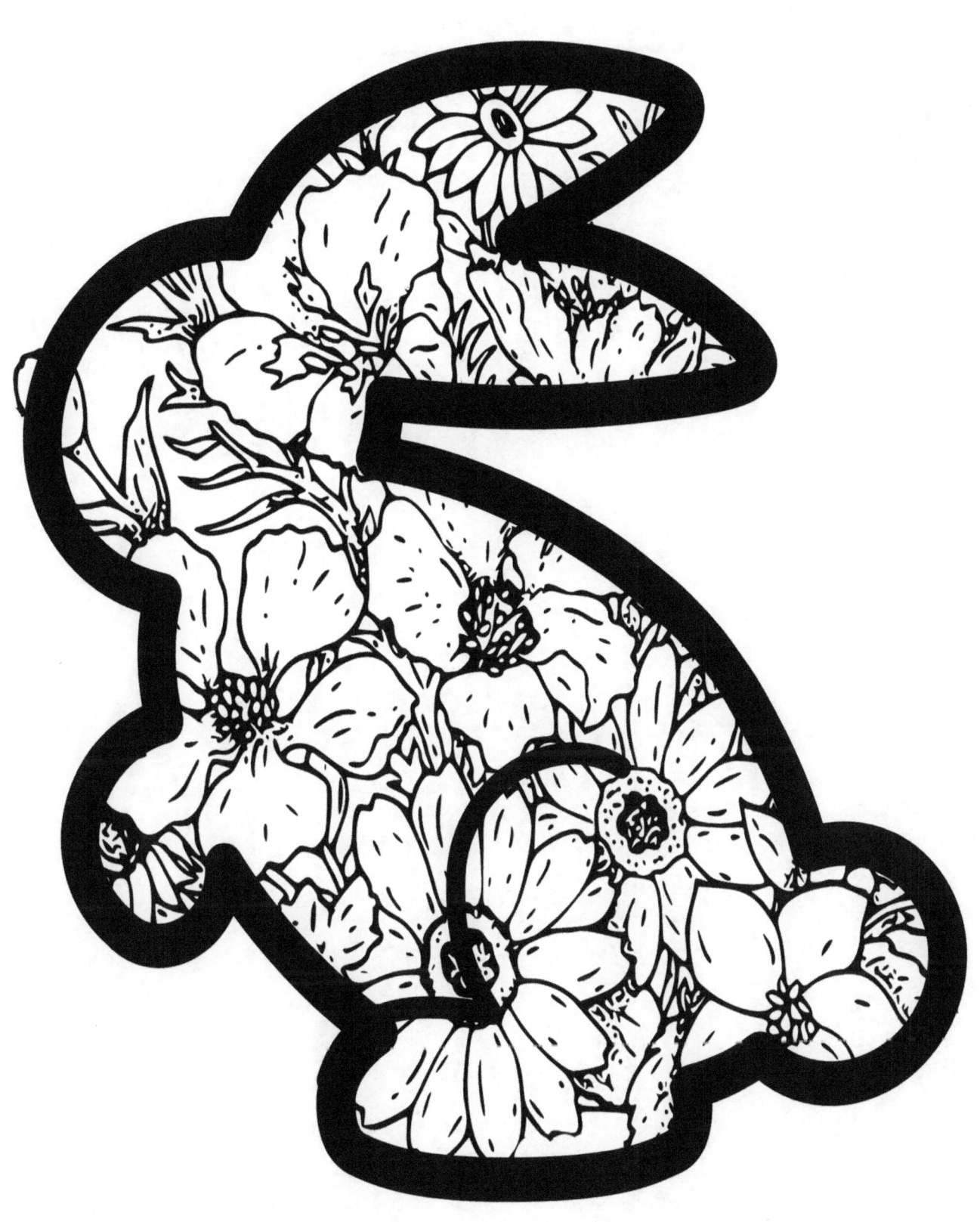

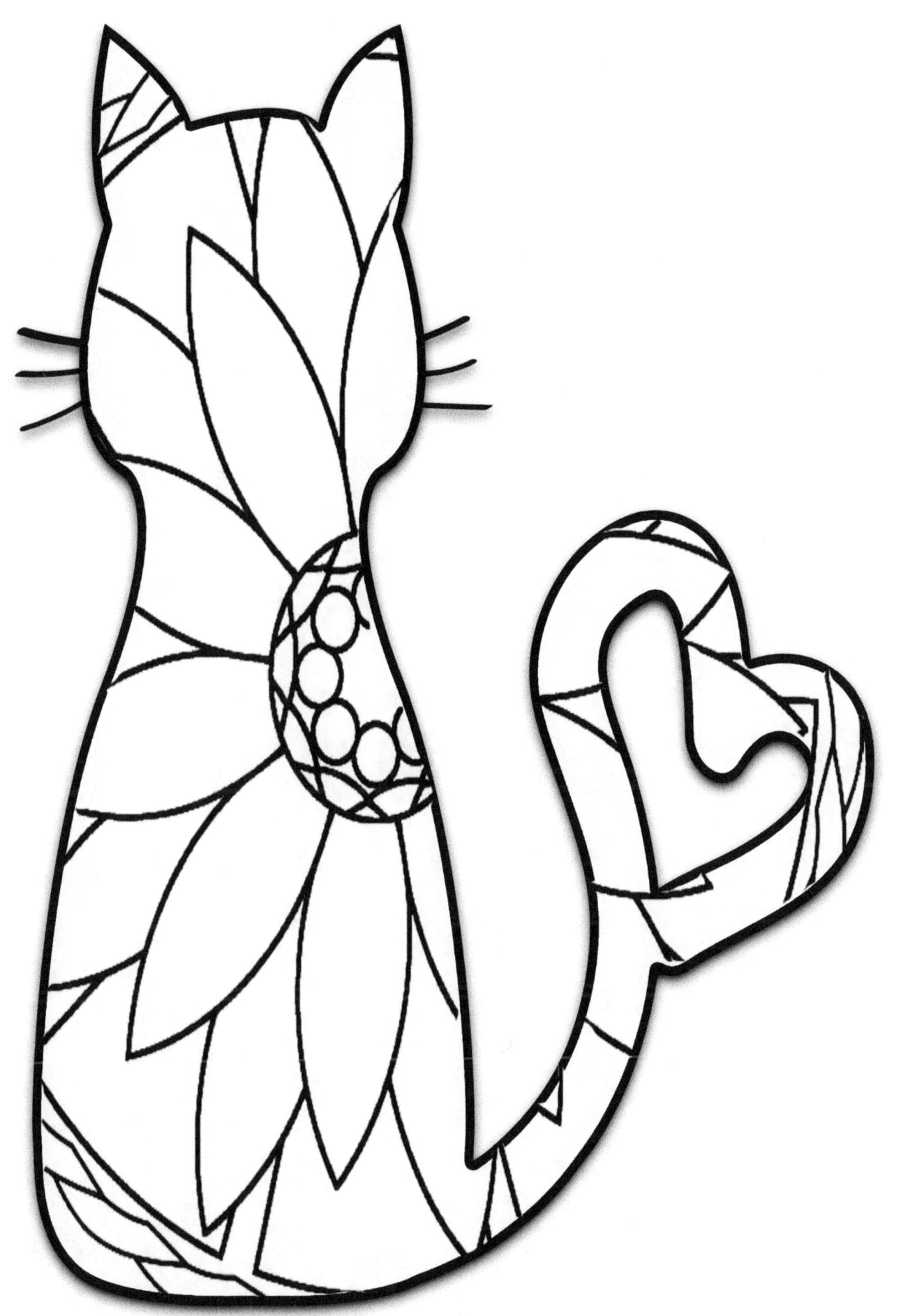

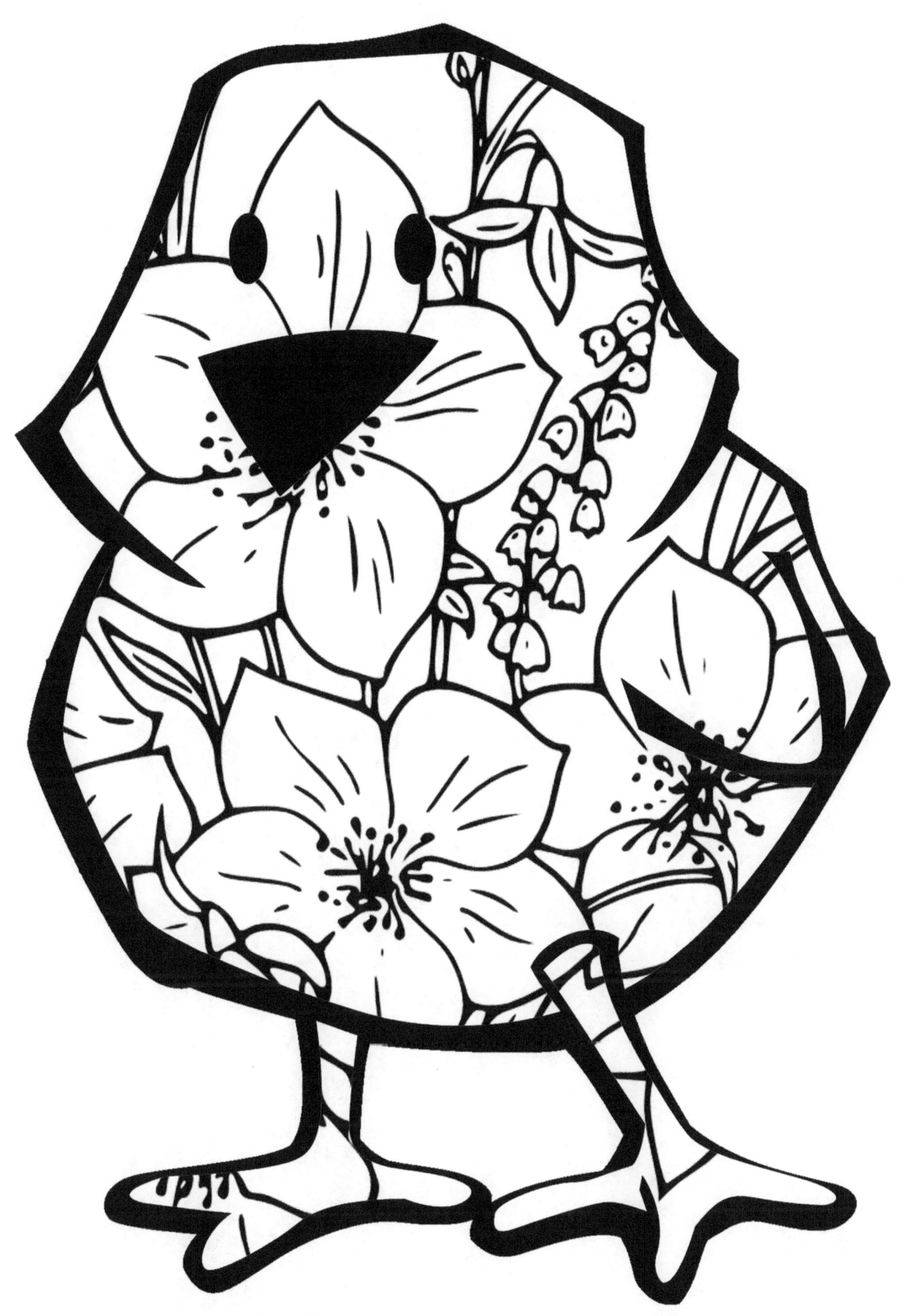

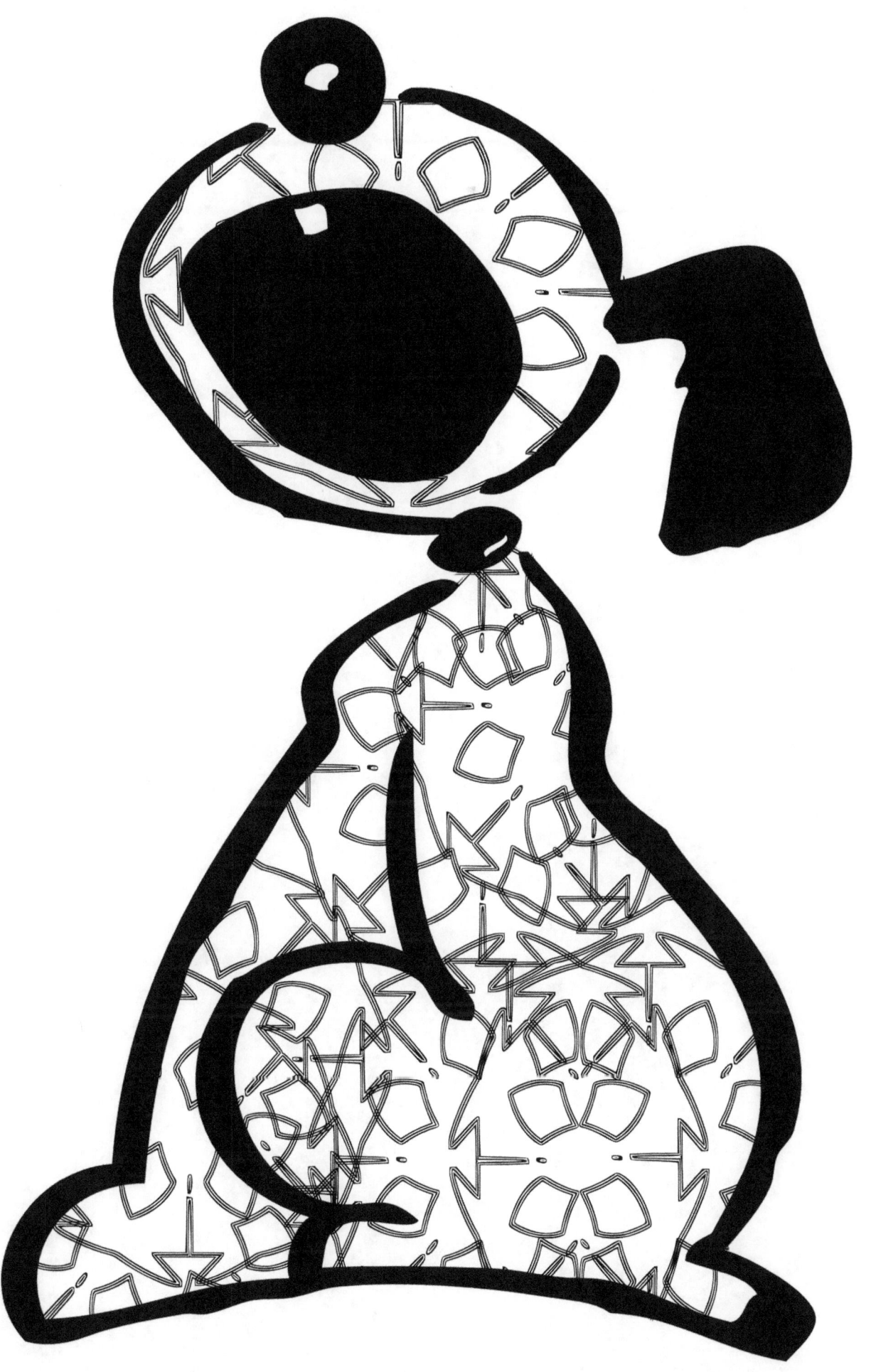

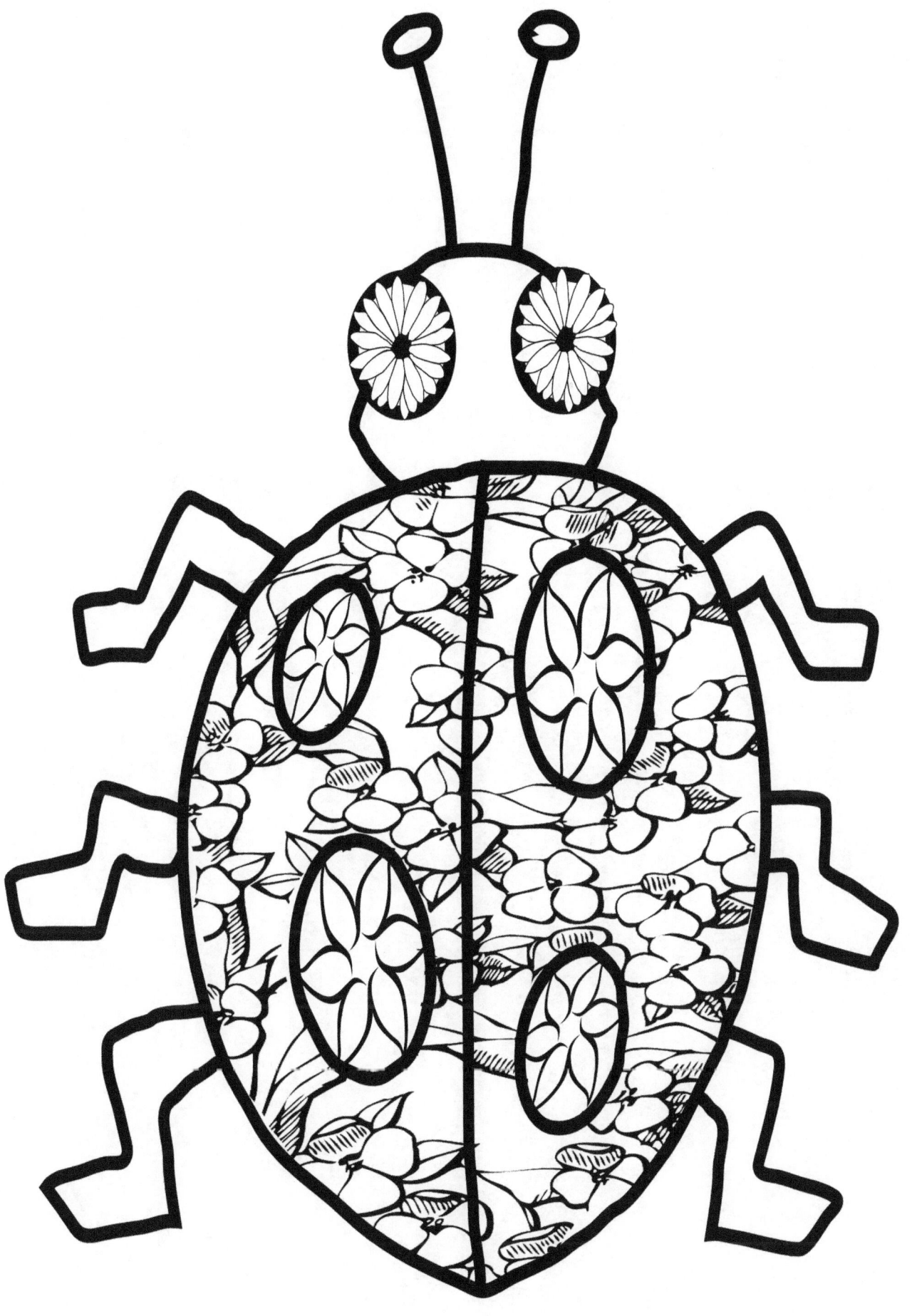

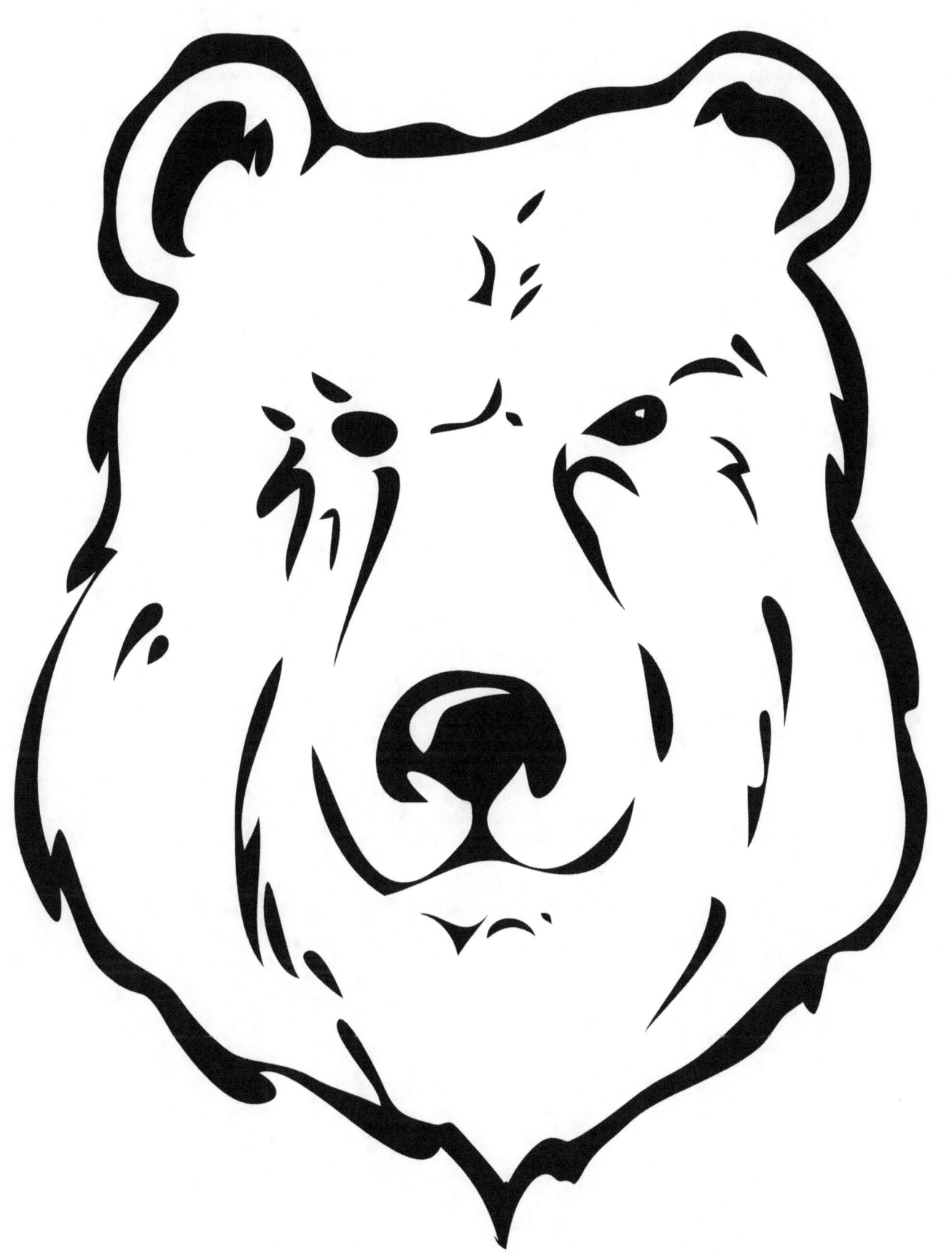

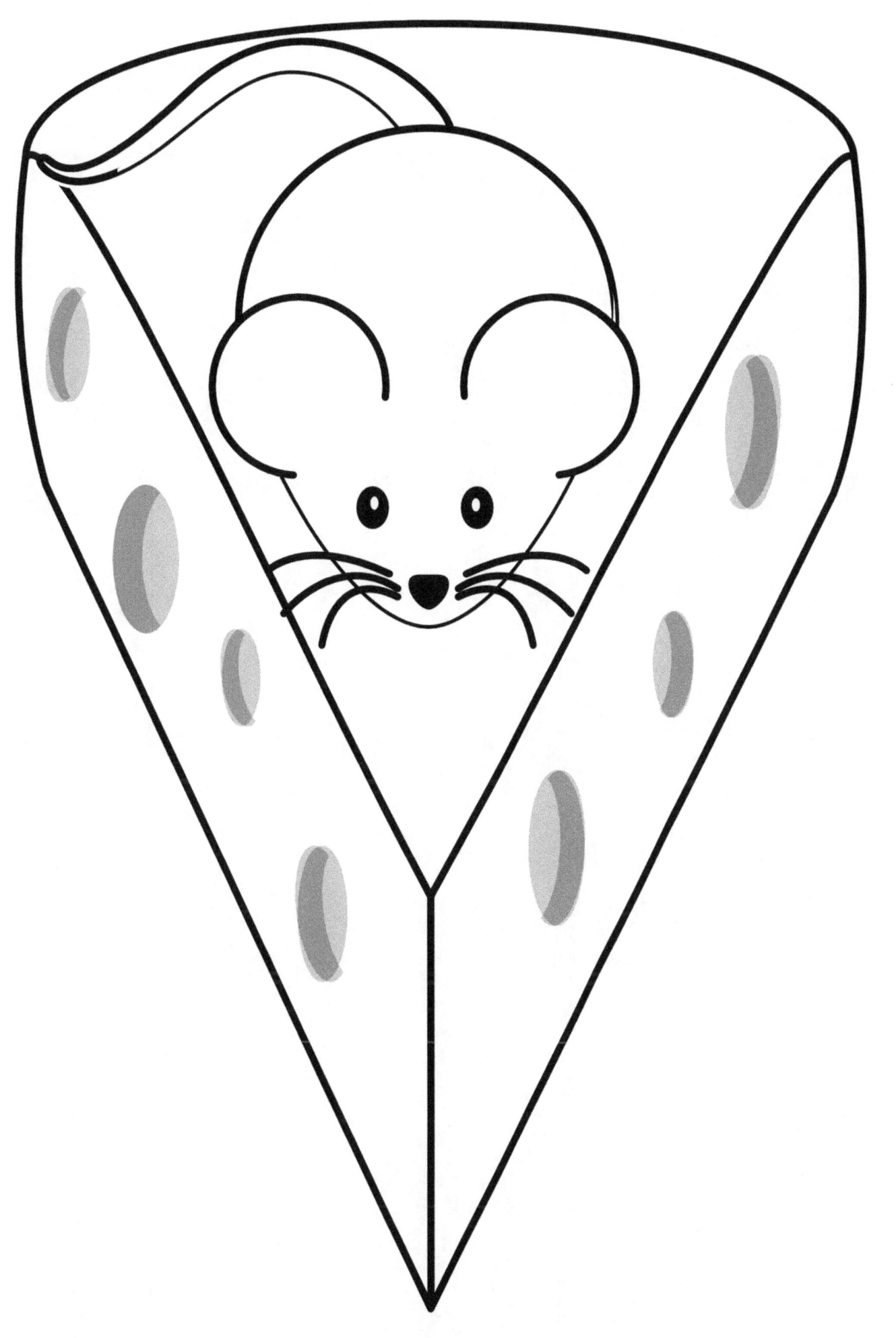

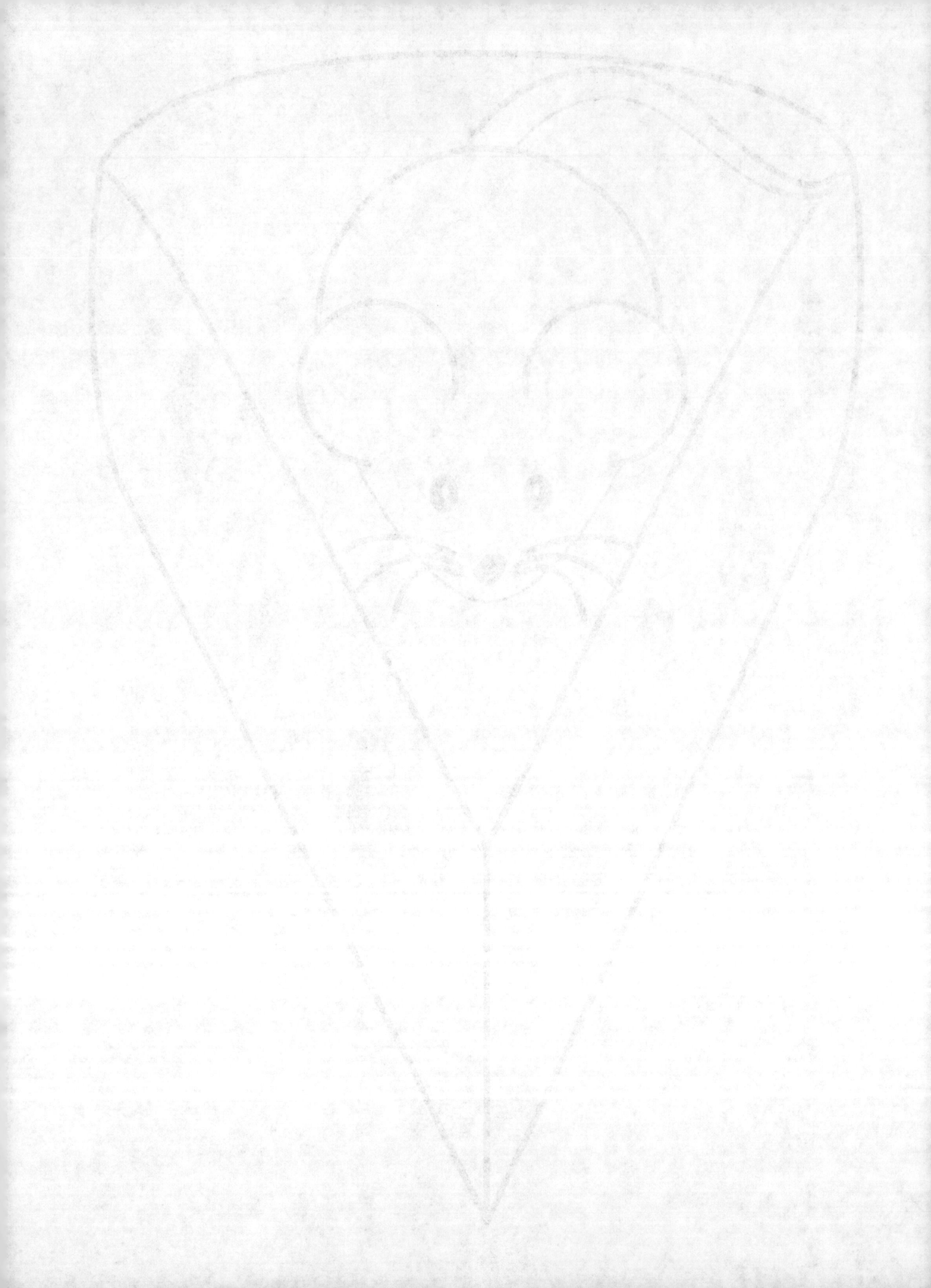

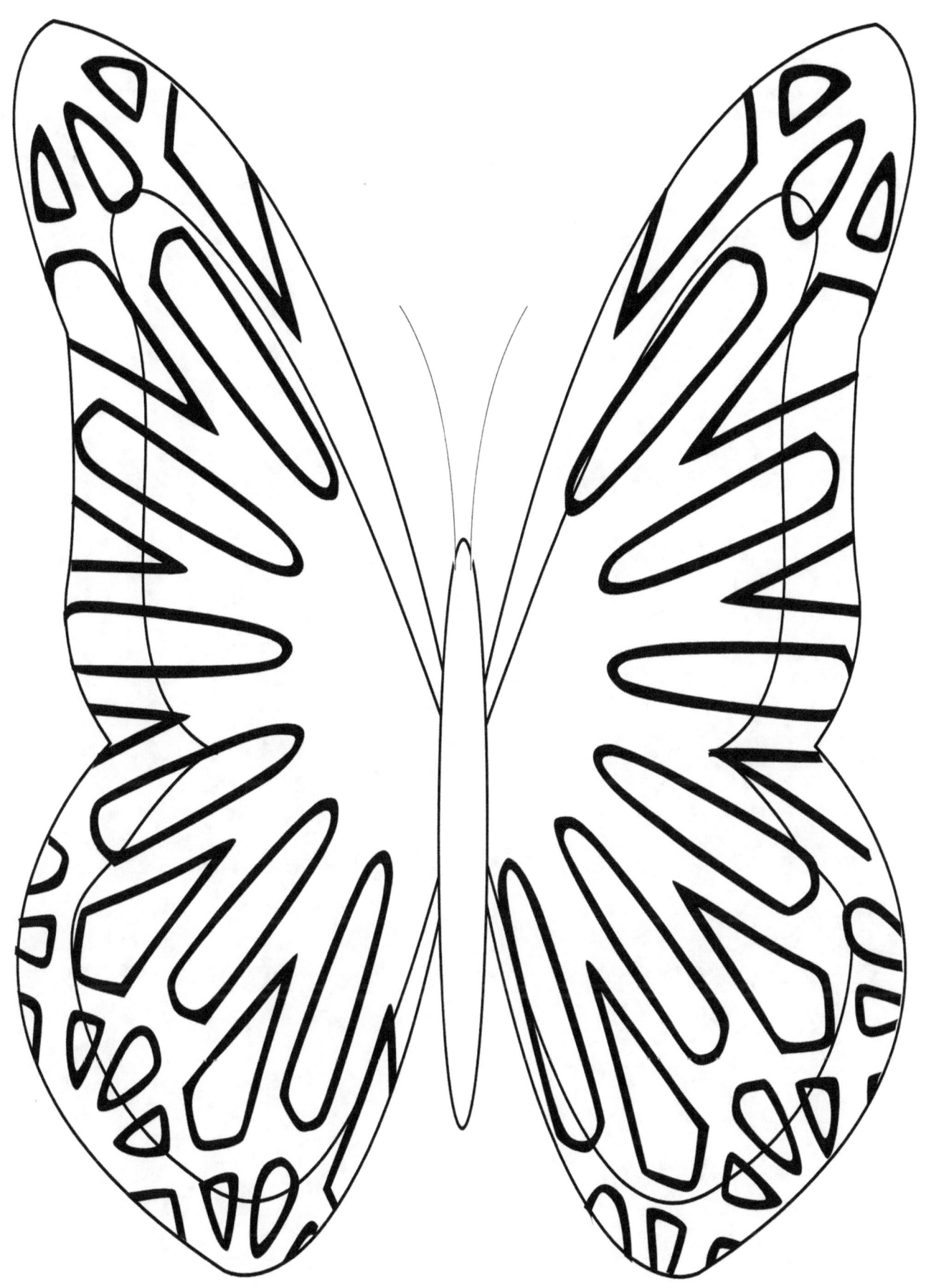

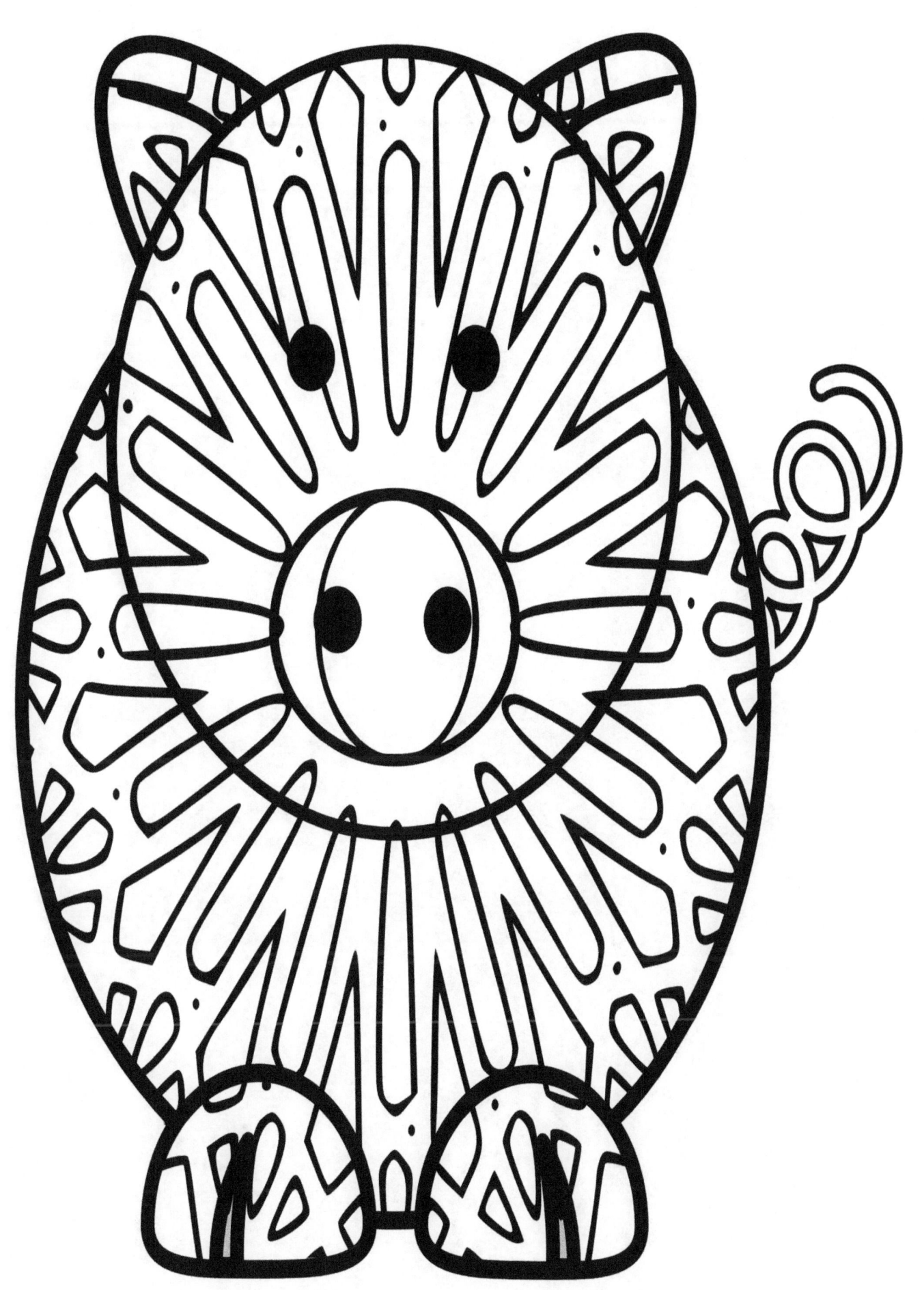

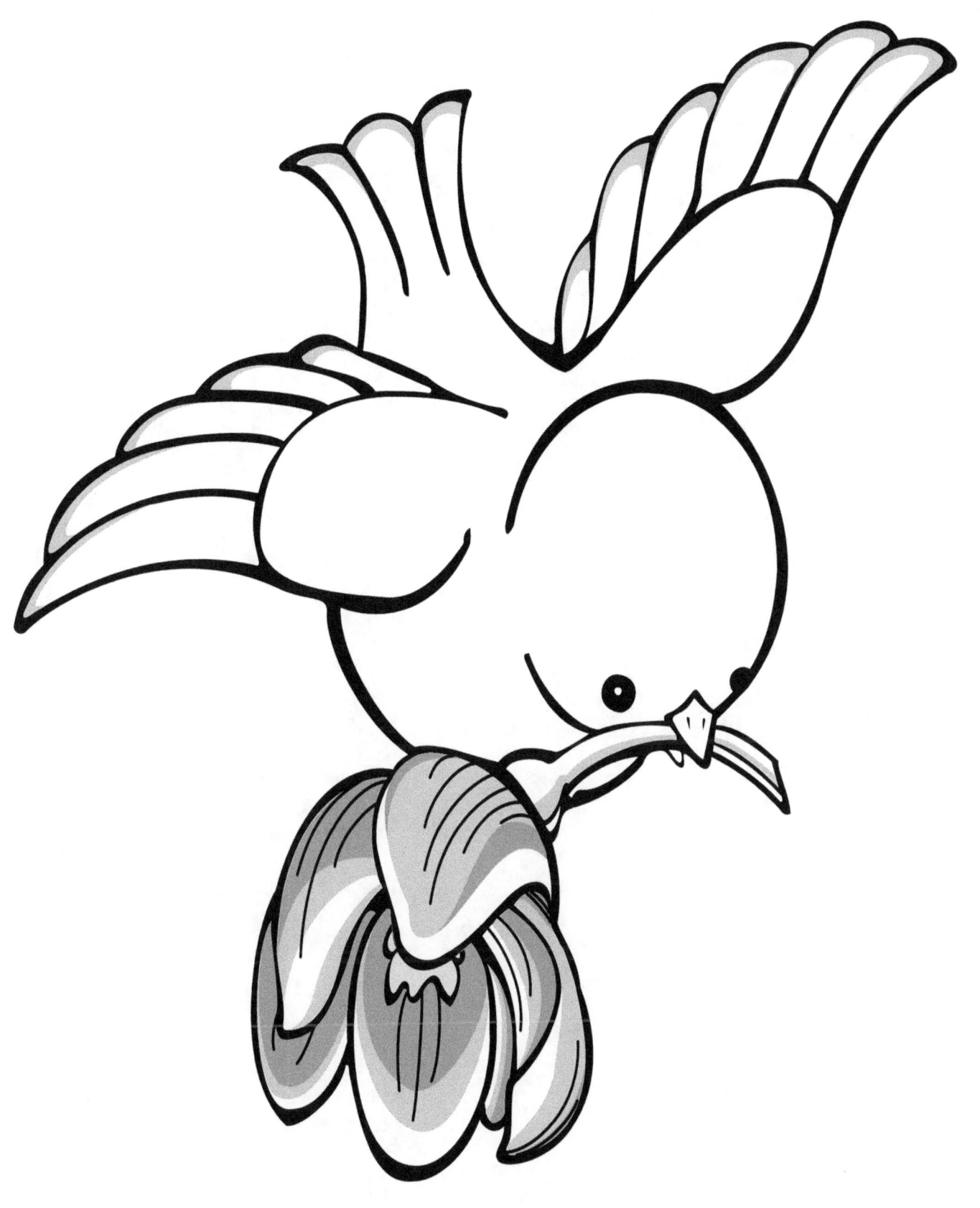

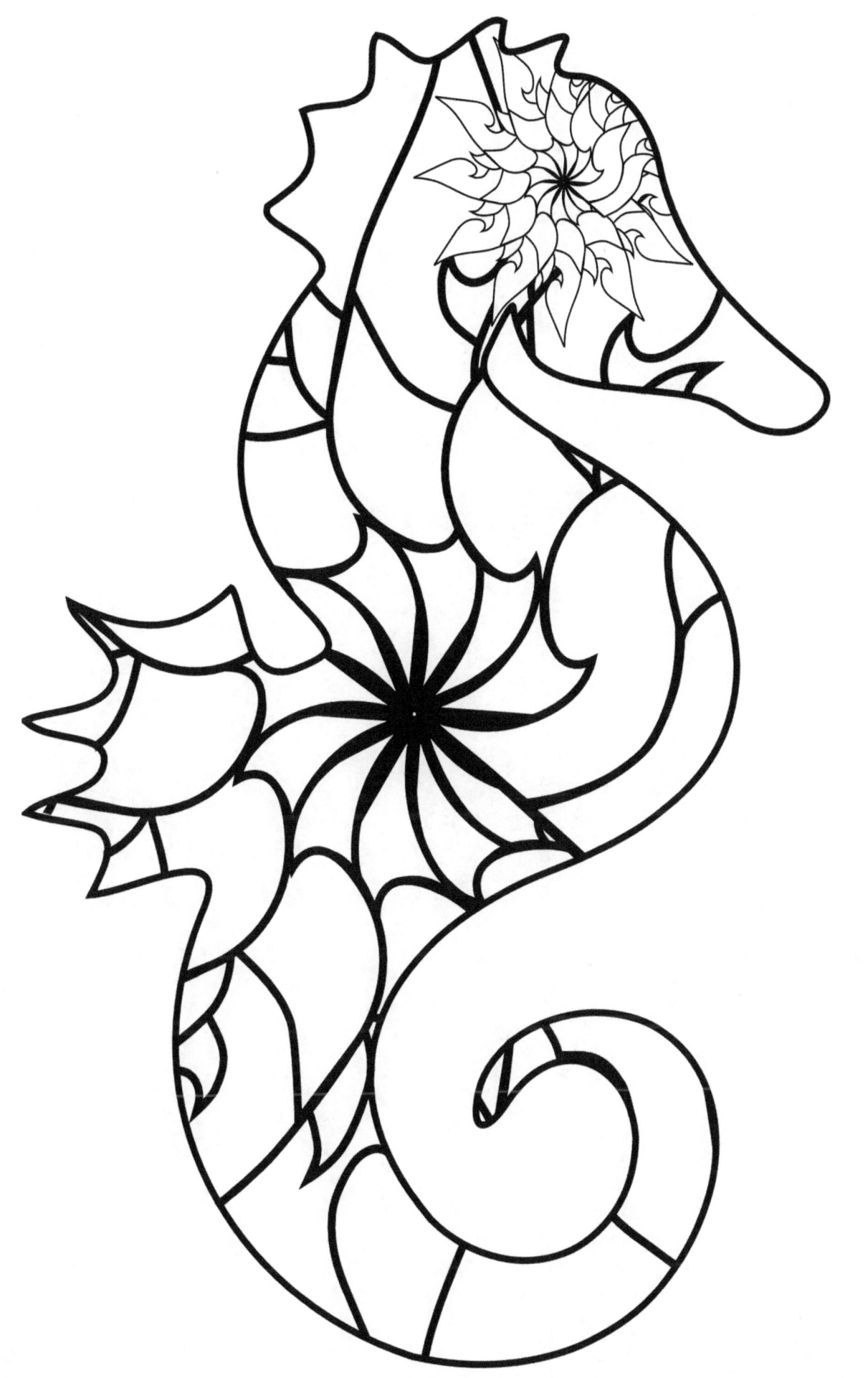

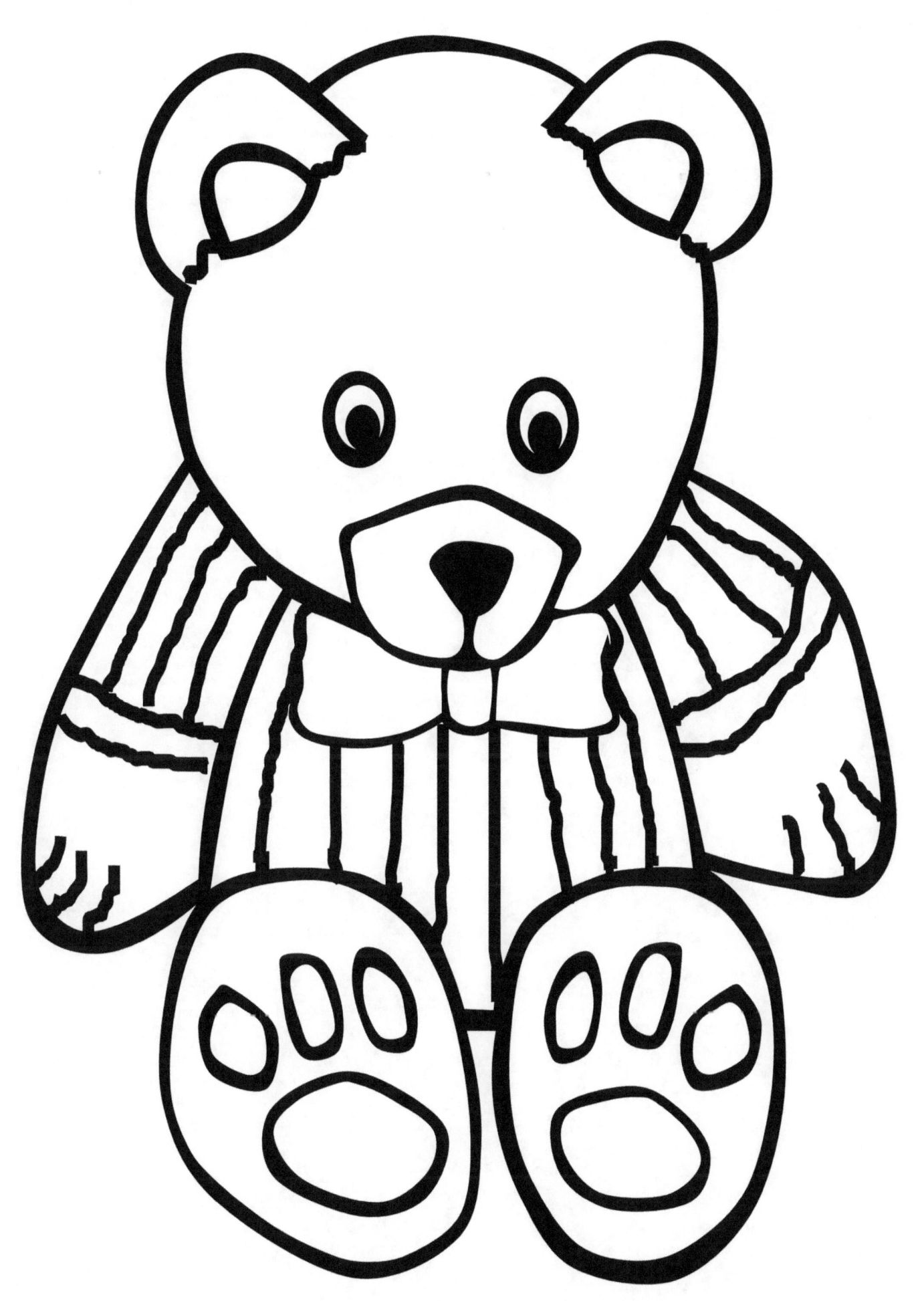

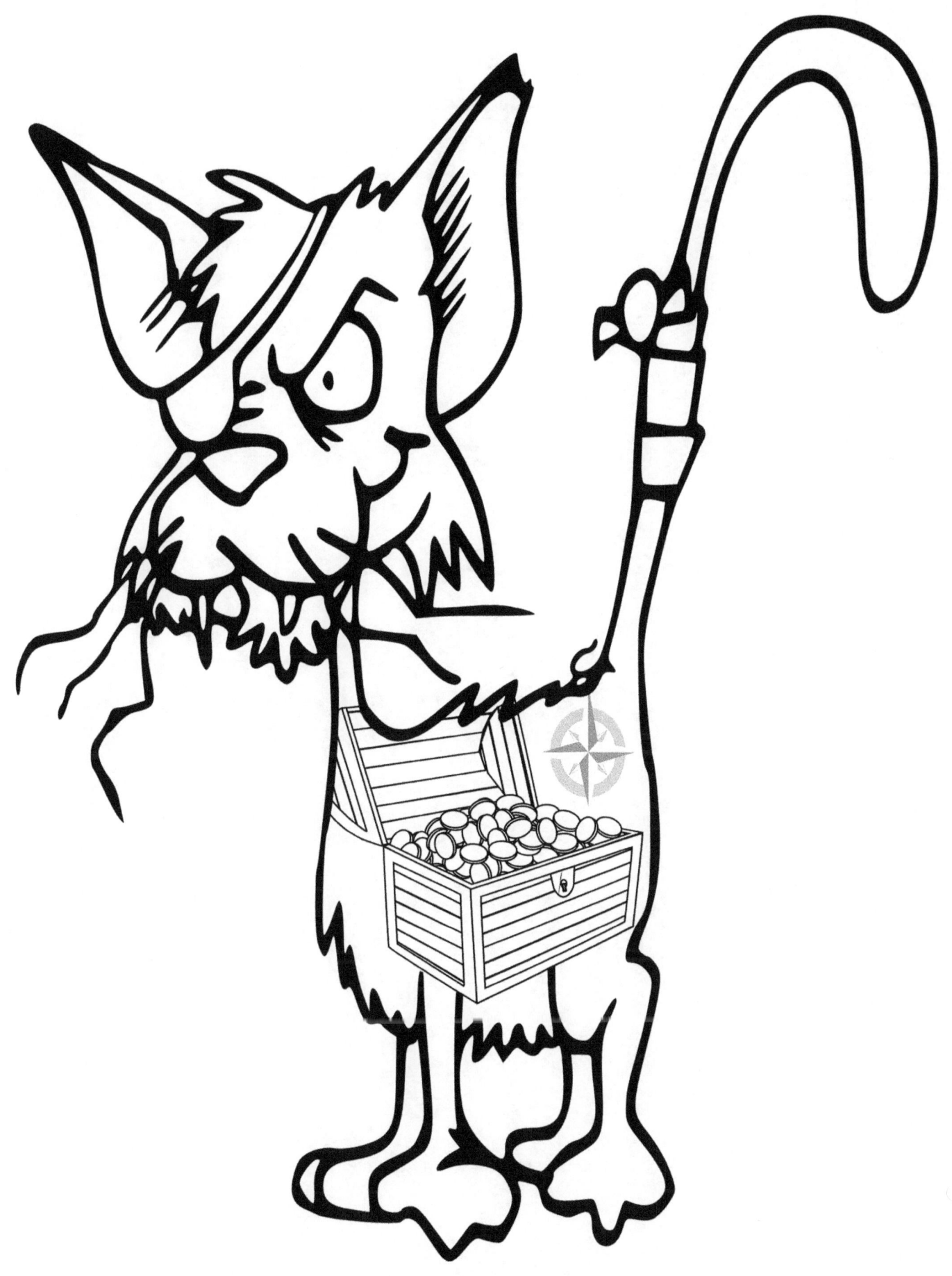

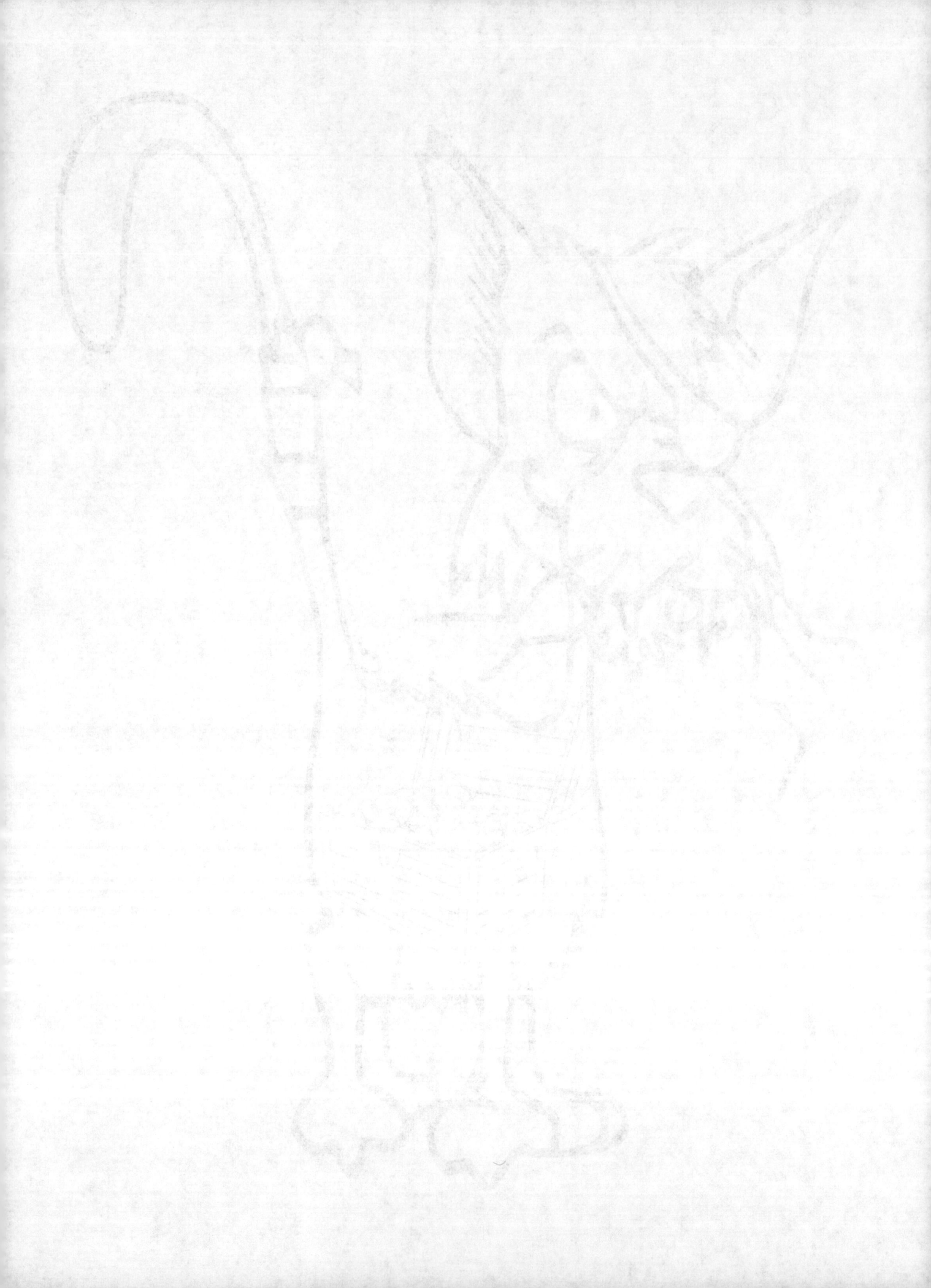

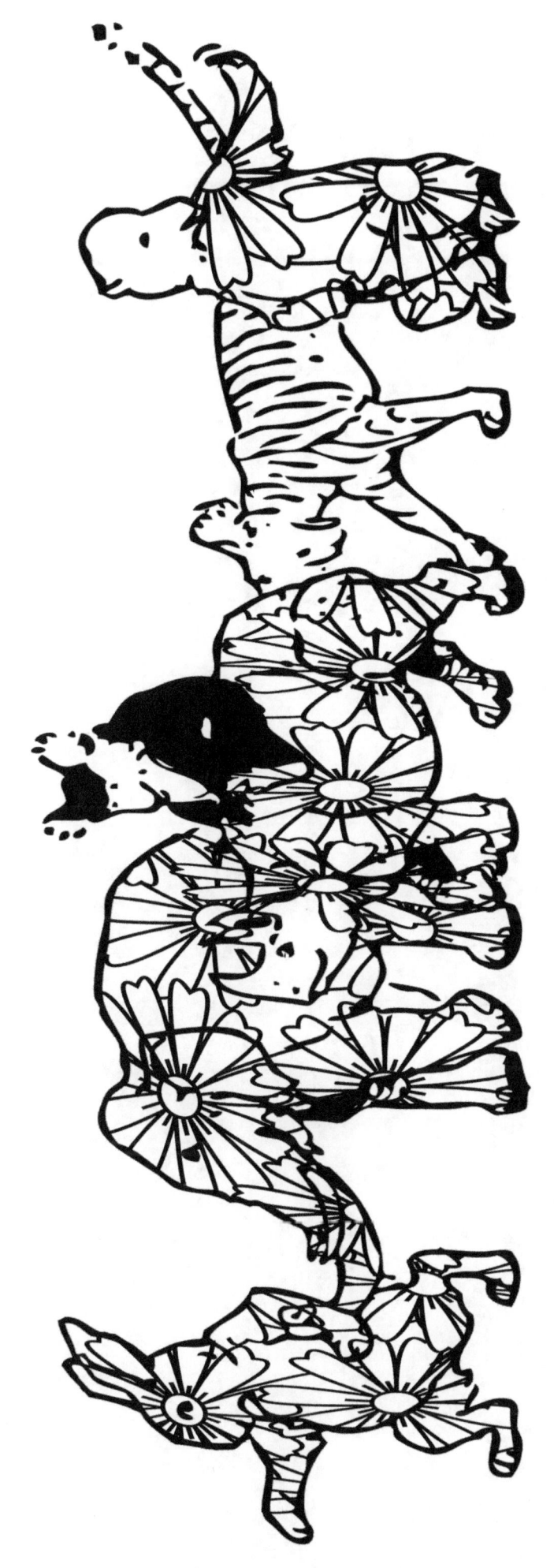

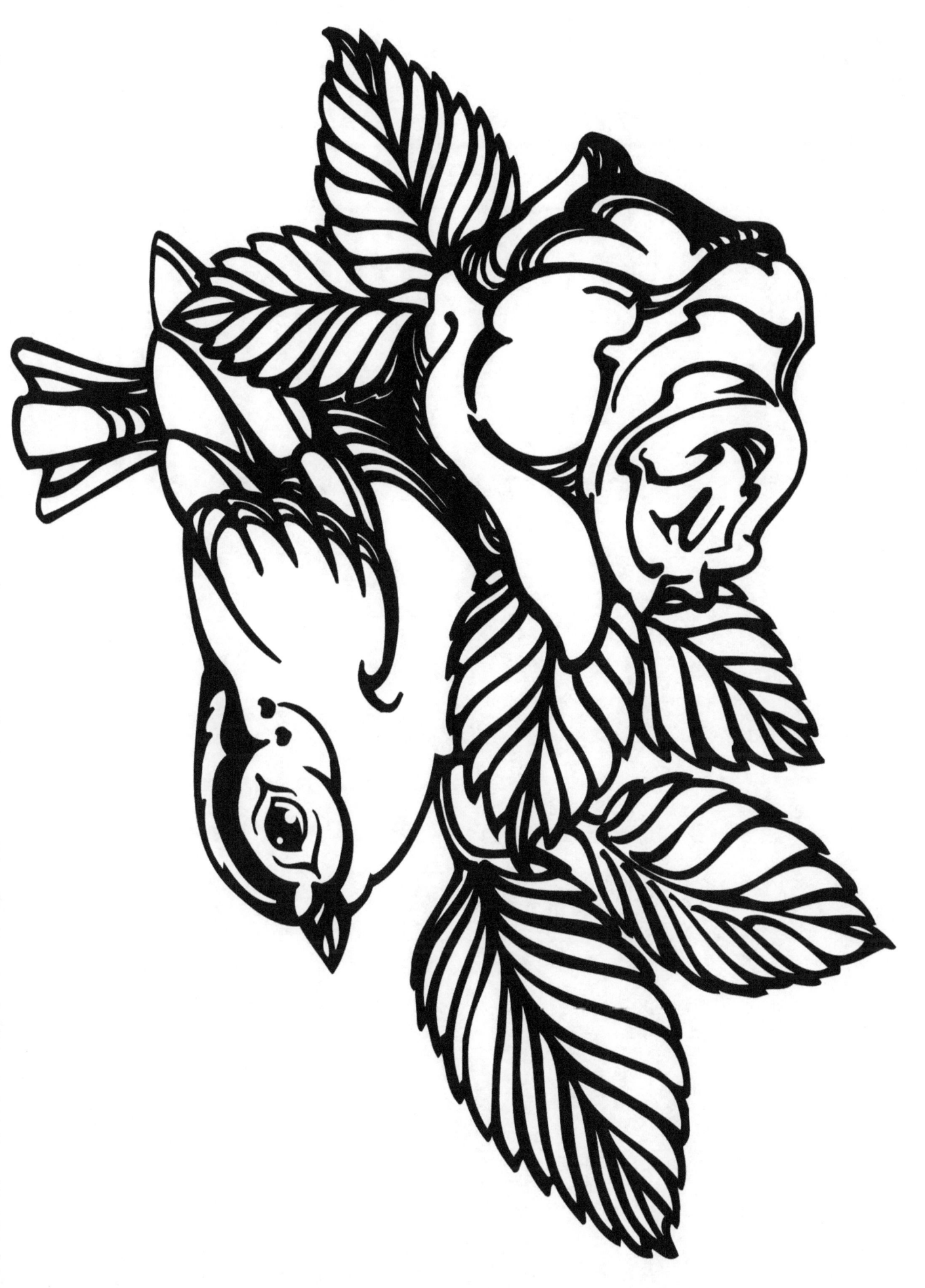

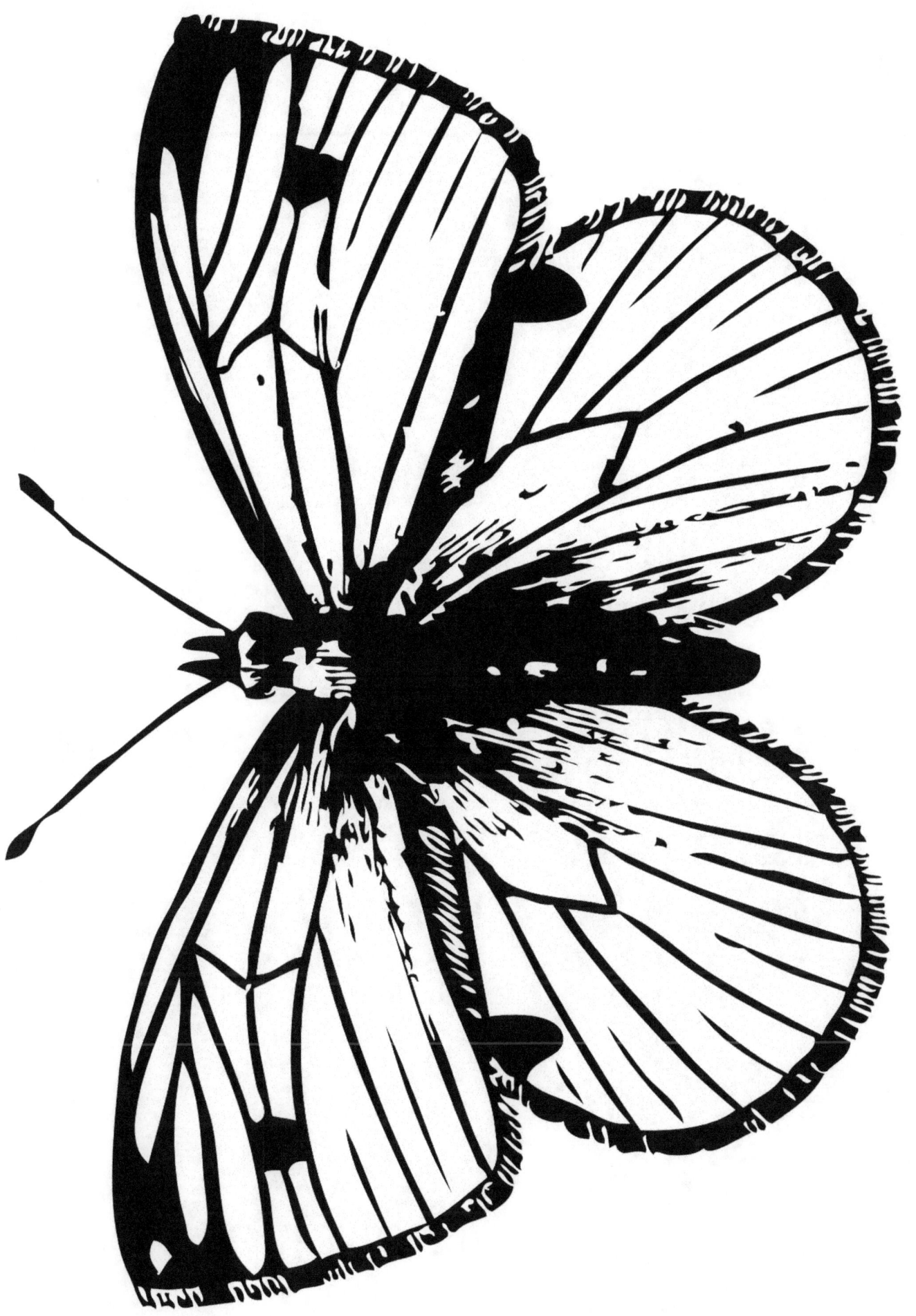

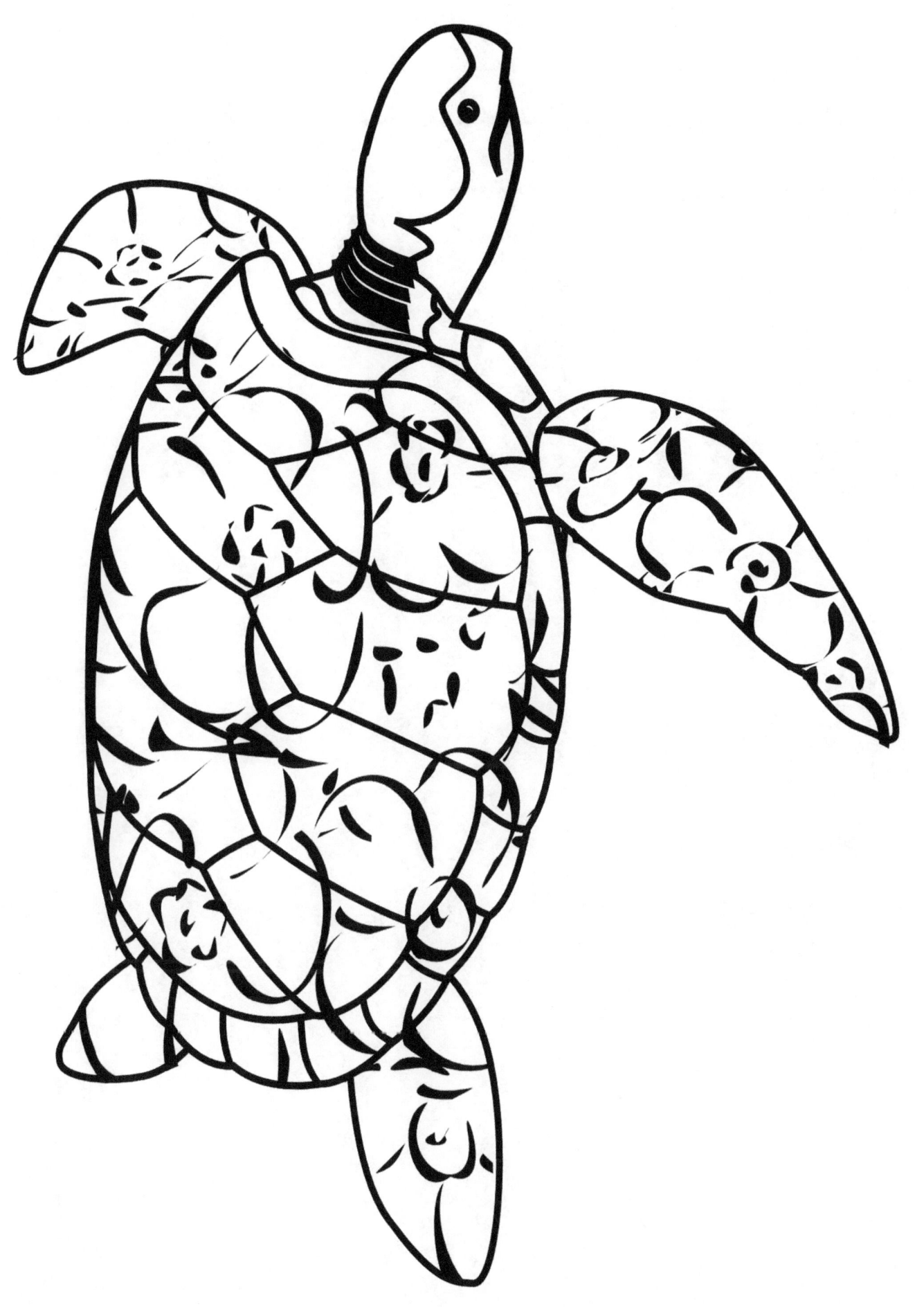

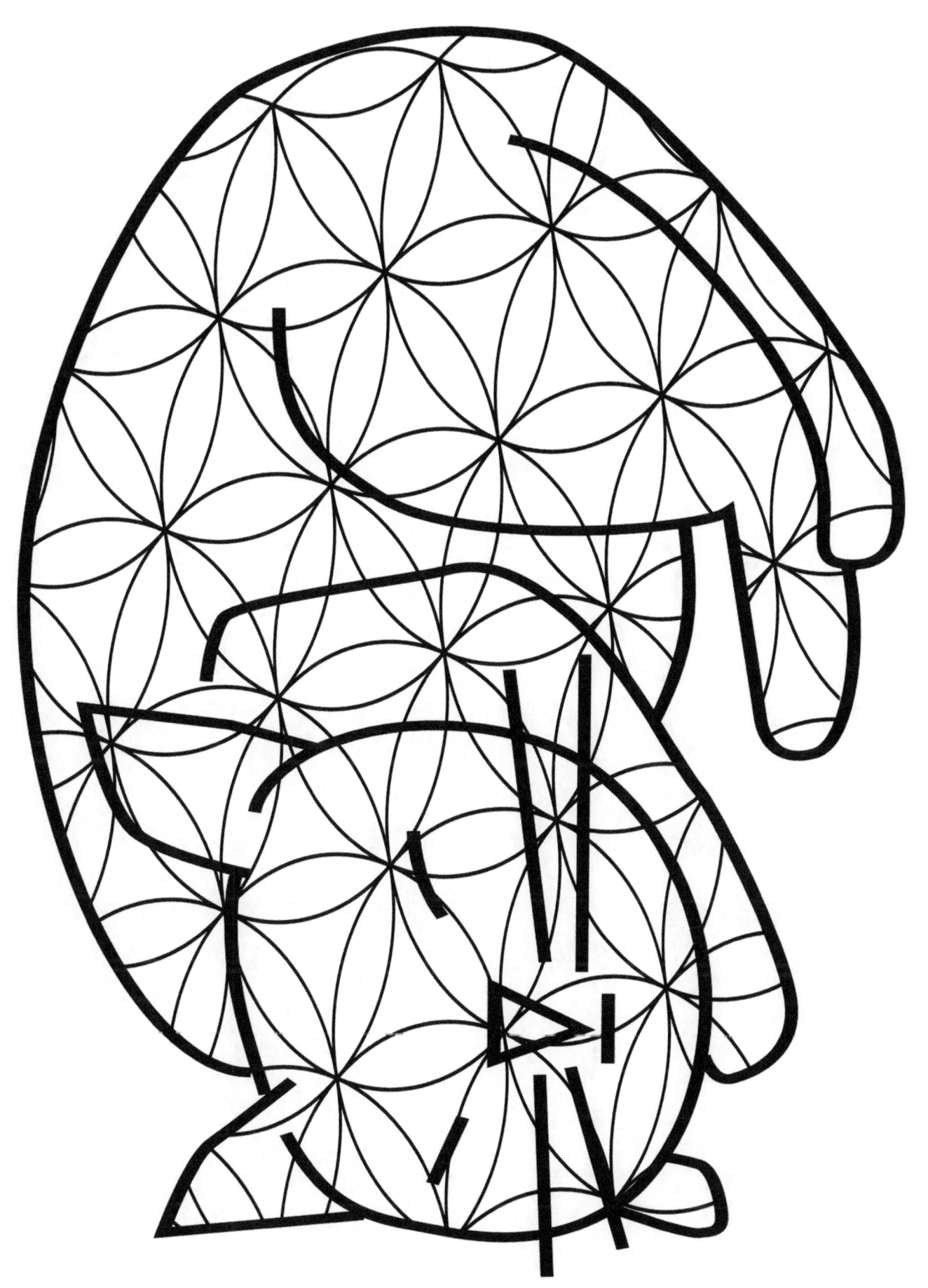

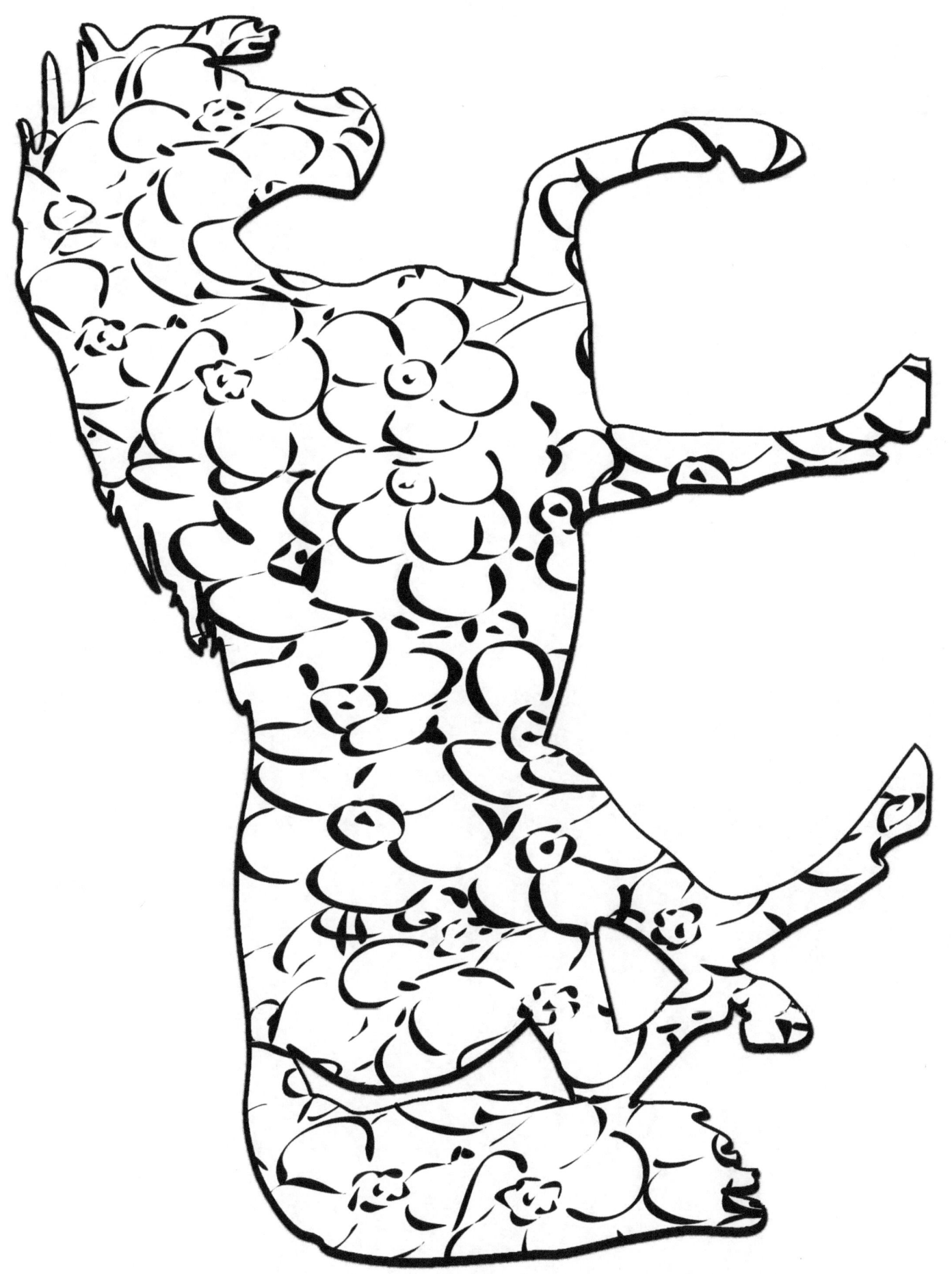

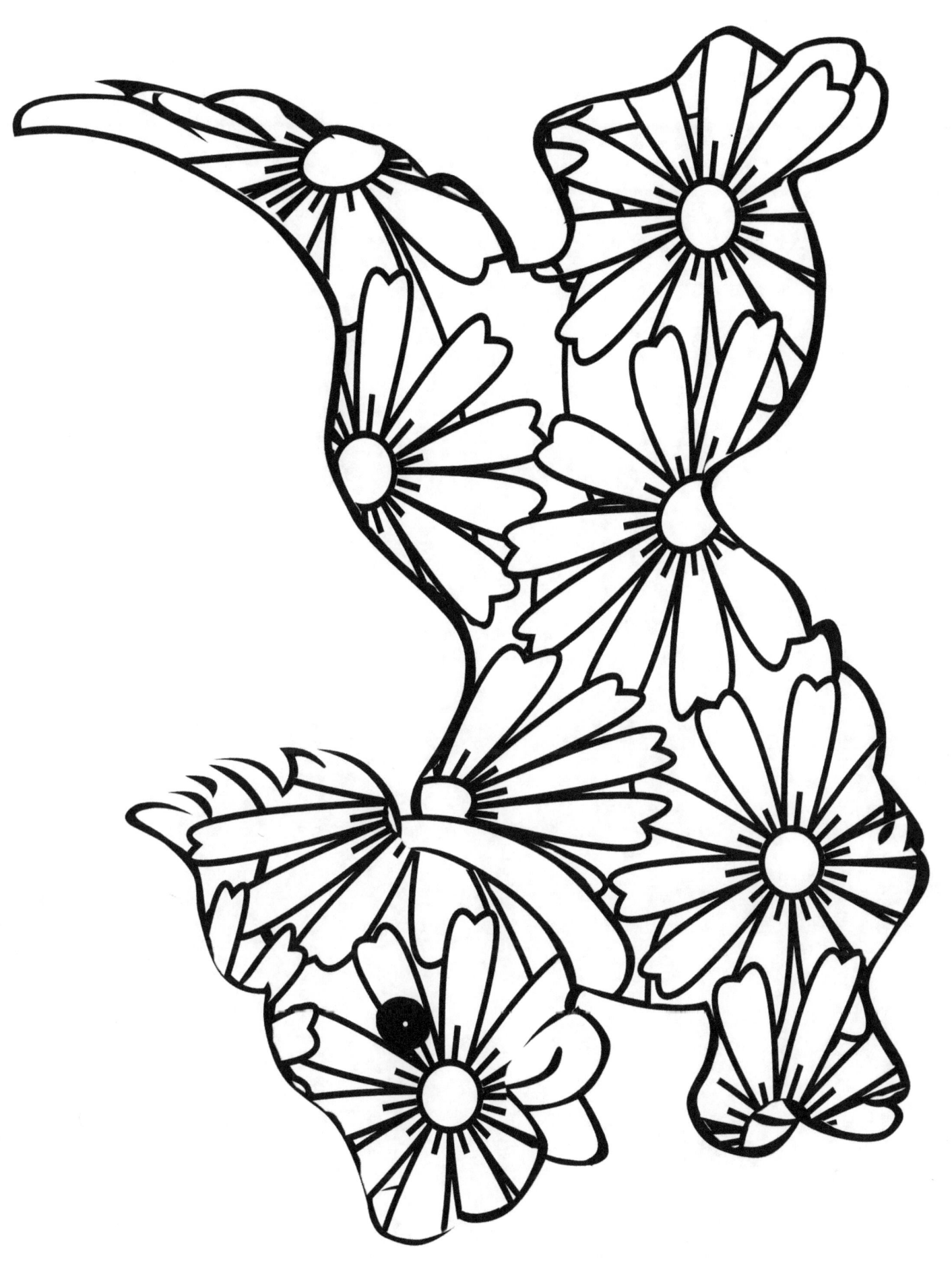

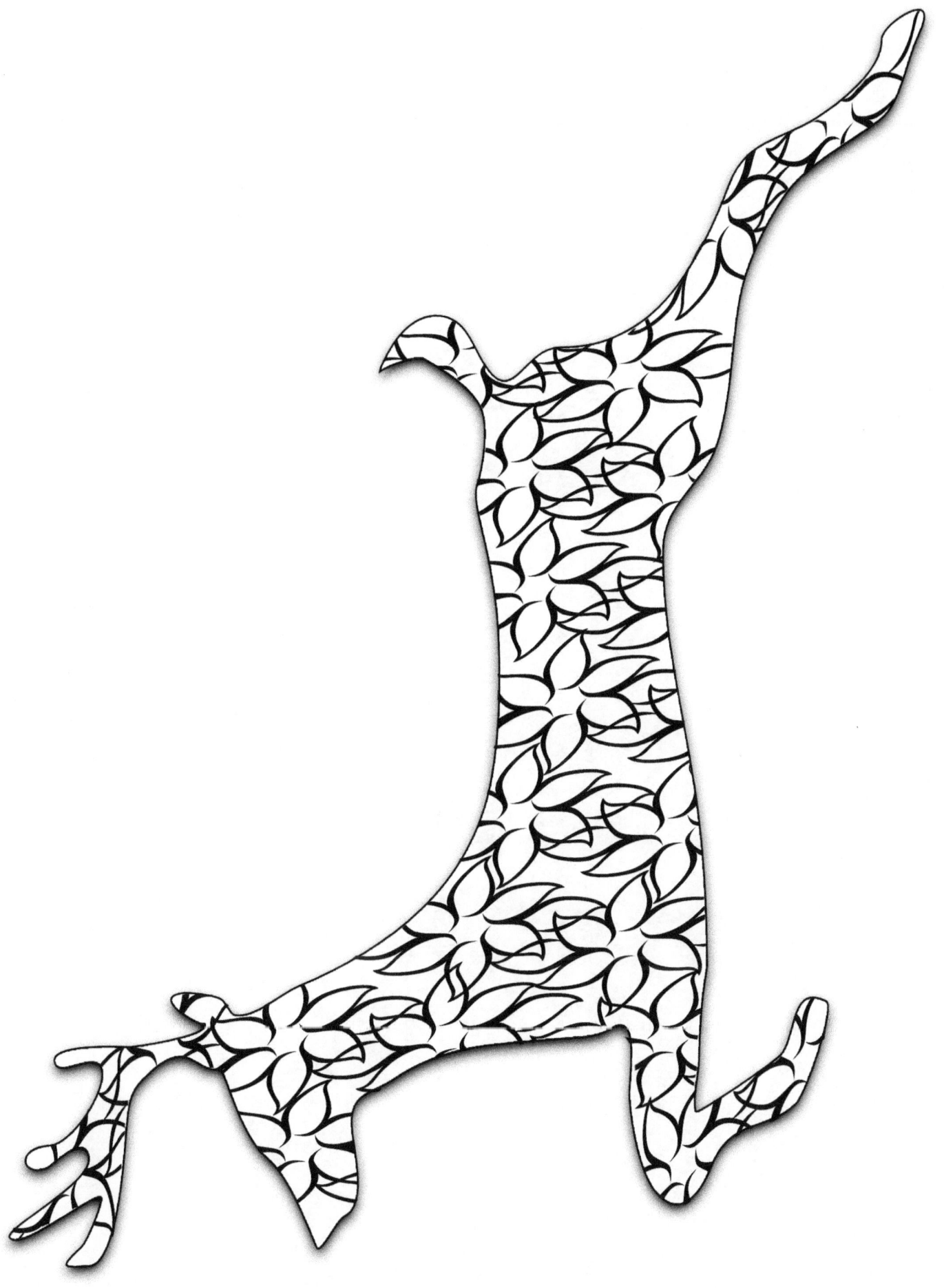

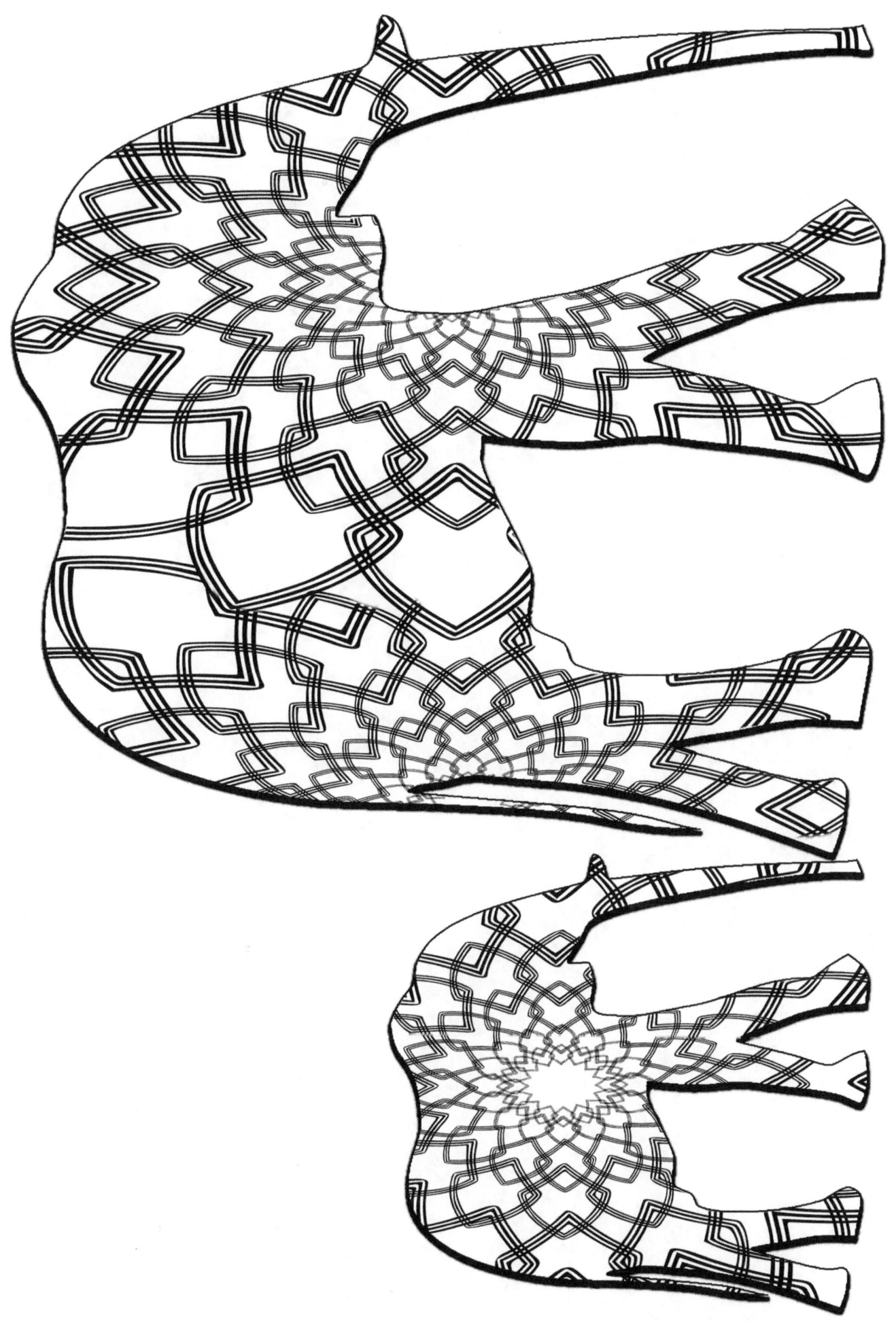

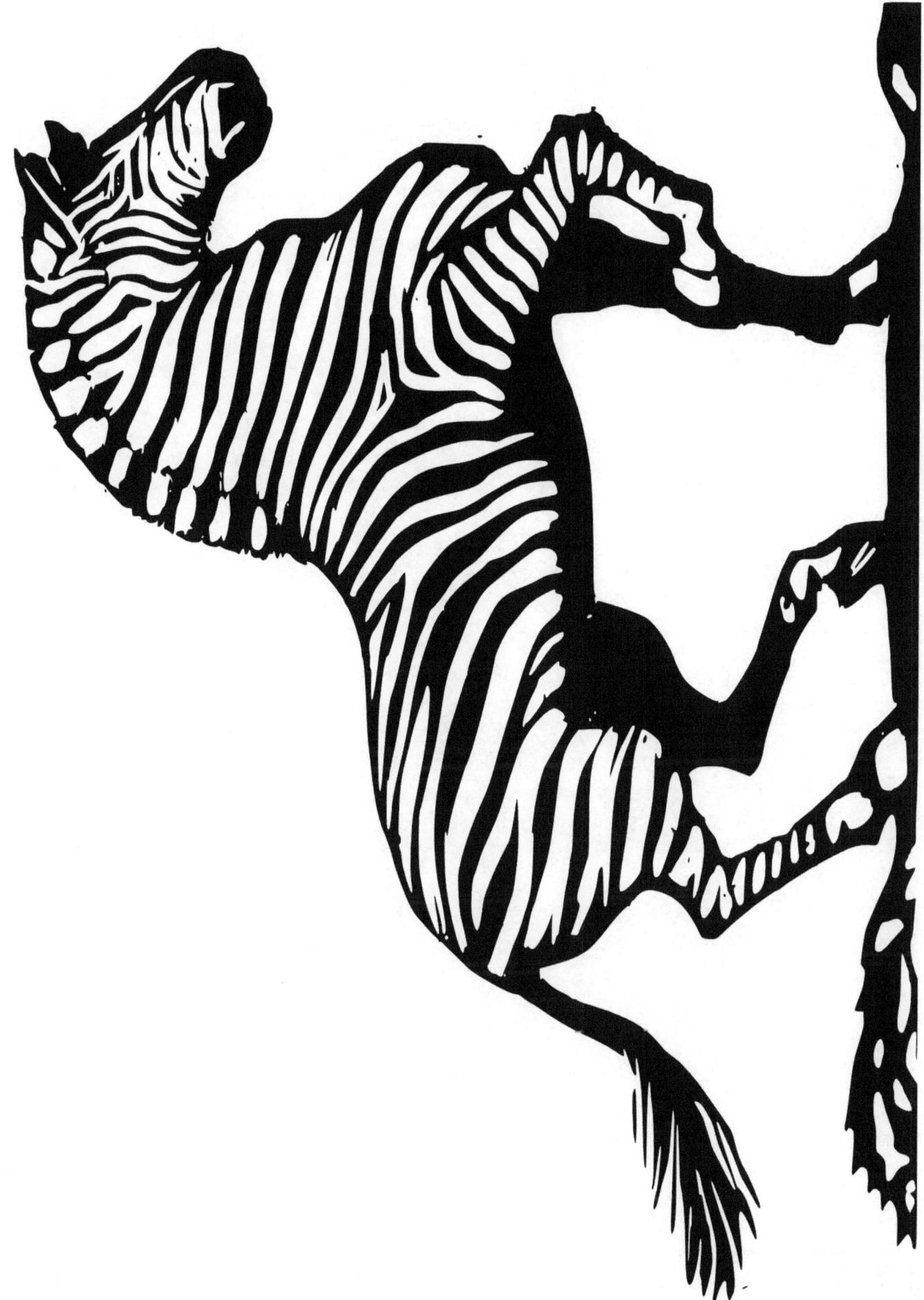